The Original Natives Guide To Freedom

The Rights Of The One
Outweigh
The Will Of The Many

by

Patrick Westley Devlin

Copyright Patrick Westley Devlin

What Is Freedom?

What does it mean to be free? Are we born into freedom or servitude? What is the role of government really supposed to be? Why is the world so full of suffering? How can I make the world a better place? What's the point, why bother?

The answers to all these questions and more will be discussed in the following pages. This is a book of philosophy and truth designed to make you think critically about the situation we find ourselves in around the world. From corrupt politicians and governments around the globe to the United Nations, the "Illuminati" (as they are so often referred to), and the corporations that have taken over every aspect of our lives, this writing is designed to take them down.

For those of you who would read this book it would be logical for me to assume you are aware at least in part that there is something very wrong with the societies of today. I would be willing to say most of you are waking up to the fact that you are being lied to. For those of you that consider yourselves to be "awake" I would caution you that there are many stages of awakening. I speak from personal experience from throughout my own awakening that coming to the realization of a problem is only the first stage.

Let us consider this. If you were to grow a large garden and each meal you harvest from the garden would represent truth and wisdom one might be tempted to eat the entire garden at once to become fully awake and wise. This would be impossible because your stomach would become full. If you ate to much you would become sick and your body would reject the food. If however you eat one meal at a time and let the food digest with the appropriate time between meals you would eventually consume the whole garden with all it's benefits.

This is the way of the great awakening. There are many stages we must go through until you come to the realization that although it is good to know our history we must learn to let it go and not let it define us. That every day is the opportunity for a new world and if you wish to be free you must first know who you are.

Once you know who you are you will know why we are here. What's the purpose? What is the meaning of life? Once you come to this level you will understand why evil exists and is necessary. If there were no shadows we would be blinded by the light.

Since the beginning of recorded history the greatest minds the world has known have all agreed on one thing. All Men are created equal. The colour of your skin, your historical background or geographical land base does not matter. We are all given the same rights bestowed to us by The Creator. We need not look to wise men to know this truth. We can know it from within ourselves that it feels good to be good. We are all children of God so therefore we are all equal. Most people in the world enjoy helping others because it makes us feel useful and appreciated. It feels good and natural to be surrounded by people who are positive and nurturing to help a society grow. The root of this behavior is love. There is a large part of the world that chooses to be selfish and think only of themselves and if you were to take a close look at these peoples lives you would see they are not happy people. The root of this behavior is ignorance. Then there is the smallest group of people who enjoy the suffering of others. These are the people that are responsible for poverty, suffering and the downfall of society. They create wars for their own benefits and have so much money that it is no longer a numbers game, it's about power. These are the people that rule our world today. The root of this behavior is evil.

So then how is it that the smallest of these groups which is a tiny portion of the general population of the earth come to rule us all and cause so much damage and suffering? They have done so with trickery, deception and conditioning over a very long time. Who gives authority to the authorities? You do, and you do it of your own free will.

It has been proven historically that slavery by force does not work long term and eventually the slaves will rise up and kill their masters. The "elite" that rule the world know this and have come up with a more sinister way of enslaving us by enslaving our minds. Like free range chickens that are dependent on the farmer for food and shelter, we are being farmed. Most people are under the illusion of freedom and feel quite content with their lives. They go about filling their days with work that some are fortunate enough to enjoy but most do not. As the chicken gives up it's eggs to the farmer we give up our hard earned money in the form of taxes. Whether it's eggs or money it equates to the same thing, energy.

    For the chicken to produce an egg it must expend energy to do so. The farmer shelters and feeds the chickens where the chickens receive energy from the farmer and the farmer receives eggs from the chickens and gains energy from them. This is an exchange of energy one might call the chicken tax. All is well for the chicken as long as they sacrifice their unborn children to their master to be slaughtered and consumed. Once the chickens reach a certain age or become unprofitable breeders they are slaughtered and consumed by the very system they have come to be dependent on and love.

    This is the way of government, however for you to fully understand this scenario you must first know what freedom is because like the noble chicken, we have never known it.

How Government Works

God created Man, Man created government. The creator is always greater than the created. This is the way of the universe. For Man to claim to be greater than God or deny the Creator would be terribly wrong. For government to claim to be greater than Man is terribly wrong. The first is not possible. For a Man to claim to be greater than God or to claim that God does not exist is like a character in a book claiming that there is no author. It is foolish and untrue.

This is not necessarily the case for Man and government. As free individuals it is our God given right to choose to surrender our God given rights if we wish. We have all unknowingly done this of our own free will, it's called citizenship.

I have always thought I was Canadian by birth because I was born on the landmass known as Canada. I always thought I was automatically a Canadian citizen because that is what I have always been told. I had no idea what being a citizen really meant or what the consequences may be. It was not until I read the citizenship oath that I fully understood what this meant.

Canadian Citizenship Oath

I swear (or affirm)
That I will be faithful
And bear true allegiance
To Her Majesty Queen Elizabeth the
Second
Queen of Canada
Her Heirs and Successors
And that I will faithfully observe
The laws of Canada
And fulfil my duties as a Canadian citizen

This of course only applies to Canadians but no matter what country you are a part of the same principles of citizenship apply. If you were born in Canada you have probably never taken this oath and believe it does not apply to you. I have brought this to the attention of others and many have said the same thing. "I have never taken that oath, it's just for foreigners that want to become Canadian citizens." This seems to be hard for some people to digest because most have never thought about it. Once you give it some thought it is very simple. To be a Canadian citizen is to be a British subject and subject to British rule. "A British subject I was born, a British subject I will die." - Sir John A. Macdonald first Prime Minister of Canada.

It may be true you have never sworn an oath to the Queen but if you claim to be a Canadian citizen it is assumed you know what being a Canadian citizen entails and rightfully so. If you were to claim to be a carpenter it would be right for someone to assume you knew about working with wood. This information has never been hidden from us, it has always been available but we were never taught it in school. When I was a boy in school we were always taught Canada was such a great country because of our freedom. "The true north strong and free" is literally owned by the British Monarchy. We are not free at all. We were all born free but claiming to be a Canadian citizen you are swearing your life to Her Majesty the Queen of Canada and all Her Heirs and Successors. You are swearing your loyalty, your allegiance and your servitude to someone who sits on a throne overseas and you are paying her for the privilege through taxation. What this means is you are swearing your very life to the Queen. She now legally owns you. You must fulfil all your duties as a citizen and obey all the laws of Canada no matter how unjust or immoral they may be because you took an oath, even if never said out loud. If you proclaim to be a citizen the oath applies to you.

Being born on land that is connected to political structures does not automatically make you a part of their political structure. We are all born free and equal, this is the will of God. To be born with another having authority over you is to be born into slavery no matter how great you think the political system may be. Being born free means having a choice as to whether or not you wish to belong to a society or political structure. In order to understand this you must go back to the simplest form of law, the Law of God.

The simplest laws and the easiest to understand are also the most powerful. The Law of God can be summed up in two words. "Be good." All of God's Law can be derived from this simple rule. This is what parents teach their children, to be good. From this comes "Do no harm" and "Do unto others as you would have them do unto you."

The problem with the laws of Man is that they do not always follow the Laws of God. Of course some laws do like murder and stealing and things such as that but there are laws that go directly against the Laws of God. As an example lets take a look at how governments treat marijuana farmers. If you are found to be growing marijuana the government will kick in your door, steal your property, kidnap you and throw you in prison. The government will label you a drug dealer for growing a plant while at the same time pushing drugs on the people through the "free" healthcare system while totally ignoring naturopath medicine and nutrition. They put fluoride in the water, mercury and formaldehyde in flu shots and spray the sky with chemicals that block the sun, pollute the air, land and water and we get thrown in prison for growing a plant that has never harmed anybody. This is beyond insane, this is evil.

Becoming a citizen is how they get us to volunteer our lives in servitude to the Evil Queen and once that is done it's time for business. This is where the "legal person" comes into play.

The government is a business. It is a corporation created by Man to attend to the affairs of the people. The ideal government is one that serves the people where all people involved in the political system benefit from being involved equally. This is like shareholders owning a company all with equal shares. There is nothing wrong with this because government needs to be managed like a business. We need somebody to organize and regulate essential services like sanitation and health care. The problems with governments is they have overstepped their bounds and become all powerful and totally corrupt. For the business of government to remain honest it must have limited power and be owned by the people. Of course all government workers should receive a fair wage but those at the top who we commonly refer to as leaders need to be limited as to their powers. Our leaders are supposed to be our servants. This is how government should be treating us, like shareholders instead of employees. In business the real power lies with the shareholders because they are the ones that own the business and the leaders of the business work for them.

Governments instead treat us like employees that they have power over instead of serve. How did they accomplish this and how do they get away with it? The answer is simple. If you are a taxpayer you are a government employee. Ronald Reagan former President of the United States of America said it best "The taxpayer, that's someone who works for the federal government but doesn't have to take the civil service examination." You can only become a taxpayer after you claim to be a citizen so you have already sworn your life to serve your master, this is just another step.

When you are born your mother fills out a form with the government called the Statement of Live Birth. There are different theories on what this is but if you give it some thought all this document does is alert the government that there has been a "live" birth on the land where they claim jurisdiction over. What happens next is another kind of birth, the birth of a corporation.

Legal person, straw-man, corporate fiction, whatever you call it, it's not you. It may share your name given to you by your parents but it is only an imitation. Shortly after your mother fills out the Statement of Live Birth the government will issue a "Birth Certificate". We are all led to believe that this represents us but it does not. It represents a corporation owned by the Queen. The birth certificate is a franchise of the corporation of Canada because the Canadian government created it. They are the creators of the Birth Certificate, they authored it therefor they have authority over it. They created a corporation or legal entity with a replica of your name on it spelled with all capital letters so that you can do business with the government through that corporation. The birth certificate is a job offer. When you apply for a Social Insurance Number often referred to as a SIN you are applying to work not just in Canada but for Canada through the birth certificate. This makes you an employee of the government. This makes you an employee of the corporation. While operating as an employee you assume all liability. Who is the owner of the corporation of Canada? Who did you swear your loyalty to? What name holds the copyright to the constitution of Canada? It clearly states at the top of the constitution of Canada copyright Her Majesty the Queen and in the citizenship oath you swear your life to her. Not only have we all been tricked into swearing our lives to the Evil Queen we also applied for a job to work for her with the title of the job being "taxpayer".

Most people think paying taxes are a necessary contribution to society. How else do we pay for roads and health care, they may ask. For those of us that understand what's going on we know the government is stealing from us. Taxation is voluntary and anyone who says any different is one of the many misled. You only have to pay taxes if you have applied to work for the corporation of Canada through the birth certificate. You are exchanging your money for benefits and privileges given to you by the government. We all have the right given to us by God to work for ourselves and keep our profits. Being forced to work for someone else is slavery. Forced tax is slavery.

Where is the government supposed to be getting money to pay for government services? Who owns the natural resources, the people, or a corporation masquerading as a government that is owned by someone from a foreign land? The natural resources belong to the people that inhabit the land. Any government that claims rights to our natural resources is a thief. Forestry and mining are two huge natural resources that we the people all own together and would be more than enough to pay for all government services with enough left over that everybody would get a paycheque at the end of the month. Governments should be managing the natural resources and selling them to companies or other countries with profits paying for health care (which means naturopaths not pill pushers) roads, sanitation, courts, peace officers (not police officers) and military.

This is not how governments operate around the world today. Governments make shady back door deals with other corporations and steal all our natural resources. The rich get richer and the poor get poorer as they pillage the land and take what they want at the expense of nature and the Original Natives. If the natural resources were controlled by the people like it should be we would not need to take more than we need to get by. There would not be the greed of the corporation who is only focused on money but instead an understanding that in order for us to live in harmony there must be balance with nature. Yes there would be forestry but it would be done in a way that is respectful and not harm the ecosystem because this is our home and we are taking trees from the forests that we live in. There would still be mining but on a smaller scale and we would only take what we need to live a comfortable life and do so in an environmentally responsible way, cleaning up our mess and healing the land as we go. We could apply these principals to all our natural resources and have enough to go around indefinitely.

    This is the way of a government that is for the people. A government that serves the people instead of rules them. This is the way that God intended us to live. We are supposed to create like God did and have our creations work for us but the tables have been turned. We have allowed our creations to get out of control and now they rule us. Like a dog that has turned on it's master, holding them hostage with threat of violence.

    The third way we are tricked into mind slavery is the democracy. I'm not saying that democracy is a bad thing but in order for it to work it must be handled properly. The system used around the world today affords the leaders too much power. Governments do not serve the people they serve the corporations because the corporations own them. It does not matter what country you are from, this applies to countries around the world.

    When one decides to become a part of a democracy it is one more level of enslavement and is designed to give you the illusion that you are free. By becoming a registered voter you are once again consenting to belong to a society of your own free will. You are not forced to vote but we are made to believe that by getting involved with the system we can influence it and make it better. This is where the illusion comes from. It gets people involved in an activity that makes them feel they have done something so they can say "I did my part". The entire political system and all it's players give people something to watch, study and fight over. It's all a wonderful distraction. They have us fighting amongst ourselves while politicians and the media put on a fantastic show for the world.

The truth of the matter is simple. When you vote you are consenting to let somebody else make up the laws you will live by. You are once again willingly surrendering power of attorney over your own life. What people are voting for is who they want to represent their masters and owners. Voting for the lesser of two evils is still a vote for evil. Prime Ministers and Presidents do not work for the people, they serve the corporation. Like a CEO or director of a company they do not work for the slaves or employees, they work for whoever owns the business. They must keep their employees just content enough so they do not start a rebellion. They are slowly tightening their grip on our freedoms and using scare tactics to justify it. They are using the media to make people terrified in order to control every aspect of our lives. The biggest terrorist groups on the face of the planet are governments and their leader is the United Nations.

The United Nations is not a creation of Man it is a creation of a corporation. God created Man, Man created government, governments created the United Nations. The United Nations operates under the guise of peace and world unification when in reality it is something much more sinister. It sounds good to most people to have a united world where everybody works together for a better planet. In reality the United Nations is just another attempt to create a one world government and bring in "The New World Order" as talked about so much by George Herbert Walker Bush former president of the United States. This is the exact same "order" Adolf Hitler was trying to impose upon the world. George's father Preston Bush did business with the Nazi's and made a fortune doing it. This is no coincidence, I won't bore you with the details, you can research it for yourself.

This "One World Government" is being brought in by first attempting to unite countries that are close together forming unions around the world then uniting all unions together which will usher in the One World Government and the New World Order. The European Union, Asian Union, African Union and the North American Union are examples that are all part of this plan. All countries are targeted for unions just as the flag of the United Nations depicts a target over the earth.

I have spent years researching The Illuminati, The New World Order, The Bilderberg Group, corrupt politicians and the evils of government and to be perfectly honest I grew tired of it because the corruption never ends. I obsessed for years researching various topics which are commonly known as conspiracy theories which turn out to be conspiracy facts. There are many untrue theories out there and I quickly was able to determine fact from fiction. I went on an information binge that turned out to be too much for my brain to digest and eventually I couldn't take any more so I took some time off to smoke weed and watch cartoons.

Taking in so much negative energy at a constant pace was bad for my psyche so I needed to take a break. Talking to people about what I knew was totally unproductive because most people thought I was crazy. Bringing up the topic of chemtrails made people look at me like I was insane when all they had to do was look up to see for themselves. It was very frustrating although I am now happy to see more and more people waking up to what is going on.

I have since decided there are enough people exposing the evils in the world but there are not enough offering real solutions. I am grateful to all those information warriors out there exposing corruption and lies to the world. Without you most people would still be totally asleep. There are two men on the face of the planet that I have never met but have followed enough to put my full support behind and recommend to everybody. One of those men is Dan Dicks of Press For Truth. For more information on the Illuminati, The Bilderberg Group, The New World Order, The North American Union and so on, check him out. As for myself I am done focusing on evil and am now focusing on a positive solution. I will caution you to be wary of anyone supporting any political candidate hoping for change because that will keep you fighting in the system. Their hearts may be true but they are caught up playing a game that is rigged against them. You can't change the system, it's not yours to change and it's working perfectly.

For those of you that may have already had your independence day, so many years ago, I would suggest you to look at your government today. Is this a system you want to belong to? Is this a system you wish to support? My grandfather passed words of wisdom to my father who passed them on to me that may put things in perspective for you. "Try as you may, you can't shine shit."

Where We Are Now

The key to freedom is education. How can we be free if most people don't know what freedom really is? The biggest problem facing the world today is ignorance. People don't know who they are. They have become domesticated chickens dependent on the farmer and willing to fight for him. This is best described by Plato's Allegory of the cave.

Imprisonment In The Cave

Imagine a cave where people have been imprisoned from childhood. They are chained so that their legs and necks are fixed, forcing them to look at the wall in front of them and not look around the cave, each other, or themselves. Behind the prisoners is a fire and between the fire and the prisoners is a raised walkway with a low wall, behind which people walk carrying objects or puppets of men and other living things. The people walk behind the wall so their bodies do not cast shadows for the prisoners to see, but the objects they carry do. (like a puppet show where you can not see the puppeteers) The prisoners can not see any of this behind them and are only able to see the shadows cast upon the cave wall in front of them. The sounds of the people talking echo off the shadowed wall and the prisoners falsely believe these sounds come from the shadows.

The shadows constitute reality for the prisoners because they have never seen anything else. They don't realize that what they are seeing are shadows of objects in front of a fire much less that these objects are inspired by real living things outside the cave.

Departure From The Cave

Suppose that one prisoner is freed, being forced to turn and see the fire. The light would hurt his eyes and make it hard for him to see the objects that are casting the shadows. If he is told that what he saw before was not real but instead that the objects he is now struggling to see are, he would not believe it. In his pain the freed prisoner would turn away and run back to what he can see and is accustomed to, that is the shadows of the carried objects. This is what they are used to, their comfort zone. Suppose that someone should drag him by force, up the rough ascent, all the way up, and never stop until he was dragged out into the light of the sun. The prisoner would be angry and in pain, and this would only worsen when the radiant light of the sun overwhelms his eyes and blinds him. The sunlight is representative of the new reality and knowledge that the freed prisoner is experiencing. Slowly his eyes adjust to the light of the sun. First he can only see shadows. Gradually he can see the reflections of people and things in water and then later see the people and things themselves. Eventually he is able to look at the stars and moon at night until finally he can look upon the sun itself. Only after he can look straight at the sun is he able to reason about it and what it is. He has seen the light.

Return To The Cave

The freed prisoner would think that the real world was superior to the world he experienced in the cave, he would bless himself for the change and pity the other prisoners. He would want to bring his fellow cave dwellers out of the cave and into the sunlight. The returning prisoner whose eyes have become acclimated to the light of the sun would be blind when he re-enters the cave just as he was when he was first exposed to the sun. The prisoners would infer from the returning man's blindness that the journey out of the cave had harmed him and that they should not undertake a similar journey. The prisoners, if they were able, would therefore reach out and kill anyone who attempted to drag them out of the cave.

This is the society we live in today. I don't blame the cave dwelling chicken people for being afraid because change hurts. It is hard to admit that all your life you have been lied to and played for a fool. That you have been farmed for your energy and given up your God given unalienable rights in exchange for benefits in a sick and twisted society. A society that has moved so far away from God.

A society that punishes good and rewards evil. A society that is run by corruption and the love of money. Where some dine every night in luxury, sleeping in mansions in their silk sheets while others struggle to feed their children. A society that is poisoning it's citizens through a corrupt health care system, dulling our minds with a corrupt education system, and hardening out hearts with a corrupt media system. The time has come for all of us to break the chains that have enslaved us for so long. For those of us that have seen the light we must once again enter the cave and free our brothers and sisters. If you can't bring them to the light then bring the light to them. This is how education is going to save the world.

Mind Games And Wordplay

The English language is a funny thing. The intention of this book is to dwell more on the philosophy of freedom but in order for us to philosophize about such matters we need a solid foundation to work from which in this chapter is an understanding of language and how it's being used against us.

In every country there are at least two languages, the language of the people and the language of government. Where I am from the language of the people is mostly English and sounds just like the language used by the government but this is a deception. The language of the government looks and sounds just like the English of the people but it's not, it's called legalese. This language is very hard to understand and in order for one to be competent in this language years of training are necessary. When we go back to the Laws of God we know that the simplest laws are not only the most powerful, they are honest. The language of the common Man is easy to understand because we usually keep things simple and say what we mean. Our intentions are clear, it is honest speech. What legalese does is use the same words as the common Man along with many larger more complicated words that they may or may not have made up and use them in a way that is dishonest. They have invented a language that is so confusing that it is impossible for the average Man to defend themselves in a "court of law" and one must hire a lawyer because the average Man has no idea what they are saying. The very idea that we belong to a society that does not allow us to defend ourselves in a court of law is atrocious. The only people that benefit from this process are the lawyers and they are all in it together. They put on a good show and make you feel that you have gotten the best deal but it's all a masquerade.

We do obviously need courts to settle disputes between people. If someone causes you harm we need a system to oversee you are properly compensated for your loss or injury. If not for this there would be people getting justice on their own in the form of violence. In these cases there would be no need for lawyers with their language of lies and two parties could come together with a mediator and a jury of their peers and state their cases. This is totally different from getting pulled over and charged with driving without a license and insurance or possession of marijuana. These are not crimes because there is no injured party. In order for a true crime to have taken place there must be an injured party, there must be harm that has been done. Growing marijuana is against the rules of the political society that we have all wilfully joined which is why we are treated like a criminal for non-crimes and thrown in prison. If you don't belong to a society the rules of the society do not apply to you, however, we must always obey the rules of life or God's Law..." Be Good".

Doubletalk in today's societies is rampant and right before our eyes. In the English language we can put an affix at the beginning or ending of a word which changes the meaning of the word. When an affix is placed at the beginning of a word it is called a prefix and it can make it more specific, give it direction or change the meaning. (happy vs unhappy)

The British Monarchy uses the term Aboriginal in both Australia and Canada in a direct attempt to wipe out their culture and further enslave the Original Natives of the land. Are you normal or abnormal? Are you the Original or are you Aboriginal? It is word trickery getting people to claim they are not the Originals of the land and accept a title within the political system. This is a disgusting act of cultural genocide that is not surprising if you know how the British Monarchy has always treated the Original Natives with residential schools, the destruction of their cultural and tearing apart their families. People think it was the Canadian government that was responsible for residential schools. Who rules Canada? It was the Queen herself and she still sits upon her throne and rules us all. She needs to be held accountable for her actions and charged with crimes against humanity.

There is another of those funny words... human. I am a man. My sister is a woman. You may be wondering up until now why I have used the word Man with a capital letter "M". When I speak of Man with a capital letter "M" I am speaking of the species of Man including both the male and female of the species. The wo at the beginning of the word woman is a prefix that is descriptive of the type of Man my sister is. She is a woman, wo-Man, a Man with womb.

When one claims to be a "human being" what does that mean? A Man is naturally a being so there is no reason to state the obvious. It would be like saying " For dinner I brought you a turkey bird" instead of " For dinner I brought you a turkey." It makes no sense. Everybody knows that a turkey is a bird so why would you say it? One would never say the phrase "Man being" however the letters "hu" before the man is a prefix that changes the meaning of the word Man. It is describing a specific type of Man but what is the meaning? God created Man, both men and women, the male and female of the species of Man. Any other type of Man that was not created by God must therefore be created by Man and therefore beneath the Man of Gods creation. This makes the hu-man being a sub-man being, beneath the Man of God. The human being is a sub-man being that is represented by the birth certificate. The human being is the legal person, a corporate fiction that is owned by the state. Foolish humans... you know not who you are.

Separating From The Flock

Now we know we have been deceived, coerced and lied to we are aware of the problem but have no solution to our predicament. There are people out there that wish to separate themselves from the government and they have been getting a lot of bad press in the corrupt media that wishes to keep us all slaves. They are focusing on people who are doing bad things and do not want to focus on all the good people that want to make the world a better place.

There is a lot of confusion about how to deal with this in the courts with a lack of understanding over the legal person and citizenship. There are some people that study and teach how to navigate through the acts and statutes to prove they do not apply to them or draft up documents of their own filled with nonsense. Be wary of these people who wish to teach you about the system because they are trying to keep you in the system. You need to sit back, put down your documents, set aside your Black's Law Dictionary and give this some thought. If you are willingly associating with a system that is corrupt and evil you are dealing with the devil. You still don't know who you are.

God created Man, Man created government. The creator is always greater than the created. If you are a citizen you are a human being owned by the state. If you are a taxpayer you are a human being that is owned by the state. If you are a voter and part of their corrupt democracy you are a human being that is owned by the state.

If you have no political affiliations, are not an employee and have taken back your life by renouncing your oath to the Queen (or state) because it was done through trickery and bad faith, then and only then you will once again be a Man. A child of God equal to all other Men, servant to none. You do not need permission from the state to drive or build a house or fish or hunt or live in peace and grow whatever you wish in your garden. You will once again return to your rightful status of Original Native of Mother Earth. You need not buy property on which to live because you already have the rights given to us all by God. We must all respect the rights of others and not trespass on the land of our fellow Man but as for

Canada there is lots of "Crown" land that is not being occupied. This land belongs to the Original Natives that were born on this land. It does not matter what colour your skin is, what race you are, where your ancestors came from or what language you speak. When I speak of the Original Natives of this land I am speaking of the entire planet. All of us are equal and have the right to live in peace as long as we follow the Laws of God. Be good, do no harm, and do onto others as you would have them do onto you.

What did the settlers do before they had the government to keep them down. They found a little piece of land where nobody else was and staked their claim. It is important no one Man claims more then their fair share or there will be trouble. Large bodies of water belong to us all and must be shared. Water is life and to deny your fellow Man access to water is wrong. Take only what you need to live a productive and peaceful life. We would then have the ability to produce the worlds most precious renewable resources for ourselves to share and trade freely. The one resource we all need is food.

How will this come to be? We have learned from the allegory of the cave that our brothers and sisters the cave dwelling chicken humans will not let us go, if we try to leave they will call for our imprisonment. They will stop us by whatever means necessary because they do not understand what it means to be free and it scares them. They will call upon the state to set things right again so they can go back to watching the shadows on the wall. They are frightened by the light and to proud to admit they are wrong.

The answer once again is education. The reason why I am writing this book is so that I may one day be free of this corrupt government and peacefully go back to my status as an Original Native. I know I have the right to separate from the government right now but if people do not understand the rights given to us by God they will believe they have the right to kidnap me and throw me in prison. If I am not a part of their society they have no authority over me but still they will persecute me and anyone else who wishes to leave the system. They do not understand that this is slavery. They would be making me a political prisoner. The only chance I have of being free is if people understand what freedom is.

No Man is free until all Men are free. So if you want to be free first you must free the minds of others. Have discussions with your loved ones, talk to your neighbors, form groups or online chat rooms. Do not get distracted by people who try to get you to navigate the system. The only way to win their game is to not play. You don't need to know their laws if your not part of their society, you need only follow the Laws of God.

Who We Are

As above so below. God created the heavens and the earth and everything within them. Think of it like this. God is the author of the Book of Life and we are all characters in God's Book. God is the ultimate authority because God authored it. God created the earth and gave Her children which are all the creatures of the earth including Man. We refer to our planet as Mother Earth and rightly so because we come from the earth and someday we will return to it. God gave Man a mind and the ability to build, progress and explore. We have the ability to advance which makes us different from all the other animals. We have the ability to tend to the earth as a gardener would prune their plants so they produce a healthier harvest, or destroy the planet through greed and ignorance. This is Gods greatest gift, the gift of free will. This is what makes the story interesting, this is why we need evil. Like all good books there needs to be conflict to be interesting. If everything was perfect the book would be boring and not much of an adventure at all. If there were no villains there would be no heroes. If not for sorrow there would be no joy. Without ignorance there would be no enlightenment. Without evil there would be no good. How would we know what good was if we did not have a point of reference of what was bad?

I was once driving home from work after a midnight shift and found myself in a horrible blizzard. Visibility was poor and the snow plows had not yet cleared the roads. The winds were high and had blown drifts of snow across the fields, ditches and roads and all I could see was an ocean of white. The road I had taken so many times had become invisible to me and I was in great danger of straying from the path and loosing my way. In this world of limbo, not knowing where I was I spotted points of reference to help guide me on my way. On each side of the road was a broken down old fence with the wire missing, a casualty of time, but all the metal posts although rusted were still in tact. With these points of reference I was able to stay on the path and and find my way home. Such is the relationship of good and evil. There will be times when your path in life is not clear, but if you have a point of reference of where not to go you will find your way home.

If we are all characters in the Book of Life then what's the point? Why do we exist? Once again I say to you, as above so below. What is the point of reading a good book? Why do we do it? We do it for an adventure, to have an experience, and that is the meaning of life. We are all the creations of God, characters in the Book of Life and by giving us free will the outcome has not been set in stone which makes it interesting. If you knew the outcome of the book then there would be no surprises and it would be boring. This is why we have free will, the ability to choose between good and evil. This brings adventure to the story and makes it interesting.

By using this allegory one might come to the conclusion that we are just here for Gods amusement and I would say to you, you are correct and this is why.

If you were to write a book and put your energy into it creating whatever new worlds and characters you wish than this would make it your creation. All of this new world is a result of your energy. All the characters both good and bad would be loved by you because you understand that for the story to be entertaining there must be both good and evil, there must be some sort of conflict, some obstacle to overcome. The characters you create would be an extension of your consciousness as we are an extension of Gods consciousness. The characters are a part of you and you are all the characters just like we are as individuals part of God, an extension of God's consciousness, and God is all of us.

When we write a book we know the outcome so there are no surprises for us, the real joy from writing a book comes when it is read by others. You have the ability to send people on an adventure, to have emotions, to have an experience. This is why we are given free will because if God knew how the story was going to end it would not be worth reading. There would be no adventure, no emotion, no experience. It would be pointless to write a book for yourself but If you gave life to characters that would write the book for you there would be surprises and then it would be fun. It would be interesting, enlightening, emotional and exciting. This is the meaning of life, to have an experience.

Conclusion

What we can take from this is only the truth and knowledge that exists in all of us. We are all children of God. All Men are created equal. No Man is free until all Men are free. Do onto others as you would have them do onto you. Be good.

We have all been deceived by fork tongued servants of evil using double speak and lies. They have coerced us into giving up our freedoms through citizenship, the Social Insurance Number (SIN) and a false democracy. I refer to this as the trinity of trickery.

We are the Original Natives and we were offered a birth certificate but in order for the birth certificate to have any affect on us we must first act upon it through acceptance by applying for a Social Insurance Number. This is akin to the serpent in the Garden of Eden tempting Adam and Eve with the forbidden fruit. The apple left alone would do no harm, it was the action of taking it and eating it that was the Original Sin. This is exactly what has happened to us. We were the Originals until we applied for a SIN and now we have been exiled from the Garden of Eden, which is freedom.

In order for us to work under the SIN we must declare we are citizens by checking a box and we are unaware that by doing so we are swearing our lives to serve the Evil Queen (or state). We have now given up all our unalienable God given rights in exchange for benefits and privileges and joined a society that has forsaken God. This is equivalent to selling your soul to the devil.

We then join a democracy that has us fighting each other voting for the lesser of evils. We are a people divided and distracted. For those that vote they get a sense of satisfaction of doing what they can to make the world a better place when all they are really doing is feeding the monster by giving it their energy.

The only way we will be free of the oppression of the government is to separate from it completely. Do not protest. Do not write letters to parliament. Do not fight them, just walk away. Once we have severed all ties with the government we will be free. Renounce your unspoken oath to the Evil Queen by giving up your citizenship. Leave the democracy. Become a non-resident. Give your notice to the Canada Revenue Agency that you quit your job as a taxpayer and will no longer be working for them. Burn all government identification because it only identifies you as a slave. Write your own declaration of independence, send a copy to the Prime Minister, the Queen and state it publicly for the world to hear. Make it known you are an Original Native answering only to God and your fellow Man.

The times we are living in now are the most dangerous times in known history. We are on the verge of living with a totalitarian world government trying to make the entire planet a prison. The only way we are to save this world is to come to terms with what has happened and deal with it head on. For those of us who have seen the light we must free the minds of our fellow prisoners and show them the way to freedom.

We are a world under attack on all sides by the global elite and there is only one way we are going to win, through education and enlightenment. The pen is mightier than the sword.

After enlightenment comes action. We must make our brothers and sisters understand even if they do not agree with us they have no right to force their will on us just as we can not force our will on them. As long as we cause no harm no Man has any claim on us. If we wish to be free and leave the society of Canada (or wherever you may be from) that is our right. We don't have to leave the land because we have a right to be here. God is the one who put us here and no Man, corporation or society has the right to kick us off our own land.

As Men, Original Natives, Children of God, we outrank all governments. We have the rights of life, liberty and property and no corporation can take that from us. If we own land bought through their system we can separate from the government and claim the land as Original Natives. No other Man would be able to claim your land and any government would no longer have any power over you. If they try to take your land from you they are stealing. We have the right to defend ourselves against invaders both foreign and domestic and for the sake of our children we should defend what is ours to the death.

If you do not own land through the legal system there is lots of crown land available that you have the rights to. You may go into the forest and build a home and community based on respect and equality. There is enough room for everybody. Everybody could have a house, garden, and a business that suits their interests without a corrupt government to keep us down. We could form a new and better government, one with limited powers. A government by the people and for the people. A government that serves the children of God and not the corporations of greed. A government that follows the rule of nature and knows it's place as our servant. A government that is totally transparent with no secrets. This is the kind of society I want to belong to. This is the kind of world I know we can create.

There would be no more poverty, no more hunger, no more wars. This would be a return to the Garden of Eden, a restoration of our freedom. All SINs can be forgiven so if we get rid of our Original SIN (Social Insurance Number) and return to our status of Original Natives things will eventually go back to the way they should be.

The only thing more dangerous than speaking the truth is putting it in writing. I know what happens to those who speak out against tyranny and oppression, they are often silenced. We must not be afraid to speak the truth no matter what the consequences may be, the alternative is much worse. For those of us that have seen the light of freedom, we must go back into the cave and free as many as we can before we venture out to start a new world. You won't be able to free everybody's mind from their chains because they have become to comfortable in their ways. Some cave dwelling chicken humans will never understand freedom and we just have to let them go. Let them live out their lives as comfortable slaves as long as they don't interfere with our freedoms. Live and let live.

Part two of this book was written first when I was studying the law of government. It reveals how the legal system works and how they have used trickery and word magic to enslave us all.

Book 2

Greenleaf's Book Of Original Law

Why Good Gardeners Go To Prison

Foreword

During the course of my life I have always felt that things were wrong, totally wrong. Haven't you ever felt that way? How did we come to this? Why is the world so messed up? Governments around the world are putting fluoride poison in the water. There are planes that spray chemicals into the air that form clouds and block the sun. Our health care system is trying to kill us. Governments rule with an iron fist. Poverty and war has become a way of life. How did this happen?

We are told to vote so we have our say in who represents us but if you do the math it works out to a very small percentage of the population that votes in our leaders and they just lie through their teeth anyway. They do not represent the people, they represent big corporations.

Our health care system has spent billions of dollars over the last five decades on cancer research and yet cancer rates have skyrocketed. Their chemotherapy treatments for cancer destroys the body's immune system and is the modern day equivalent to being burnt at the stake.

They have known all along that cancer is a fungus and can be treated by consuming large amounts of organic vegetables and fruits due to their natural anti-fungal properties. The pesticides and fungicides being sprayed on the majority of today's crops change the plants chemically because the plants no longer need to create a chemical called "salvestrols" that kills fungi naturally. The cure for cancer. But there's no money in that.

The government that runs our health care system is pushing vaccines on its public that contain mercury and formaldehyde which are toxic poisons. Your general practitioner doctor is no more than a drug pusher for the pharmaceutical cartels. The superpowers of the world are spreading democracy, which is supposed to be a good thing, by invading other countries and killing people. How did we come to this? Just what the hell is going on?

The answer is simple, we allowed it to happen so it did. True you were tricked into playing their game because we have been conditioned for a very long time, we thought that we had to, that it's just the way the world works. You asked to be a part of their system, you were not forced. At least not in the so called free societies of democracy. The majority of Canadians probably don't realize if you have a Social Insurance Number and pay taxes you are considered a government agent employed by Her Majesty the Queen.

You probably don't know what citizenship, the birth certificate or a democracy really is, but you do know something is wrong, very wrong indeed.

There is simply too much to cover in one book and I wanted to keep this short and simple so I have decided to stick to a few basic topics, otherwise I would never finish. This will not be a history lesson or a book on what bad people do or what their motives might be.

This will be a book about you.

In The Beginning

Since the beginning of our known history the greatest scholars have come to the same conclusion, that we are a part of something bigger. There is something that brought us to be, something that made us. Whether you call this God, The Great Spirit or any other name or belief system you may have, the majority of the people on the planet believe in something greater than ourselves.

It is true there are many people that believe in nothing, that we are just an accident, a fluke in time, that there is no God. That's O.K. I am not here to push any belief systems on anybody. To each their own as long as you do no harm. It's your right to be wrong. All I will say is this. If you wish to see God you need only look into the eyes of a child.

When you were born, no matter what geographical country you arrived in upon exiting the womb, you were born free. Equal to all Men with no other Man having authority over you.

Before I continue I think I should clarify that when I speak of Man I am referring to both the male and female of the species of Man. For greater clarification I think you may need to understand more about how the English language works. For all the females out there reading this book who are thinking "I'm not a man I'm a woman!" You need to give this some thought.

True you are a woman, but you are also a Man. When I speak of Man in a certain context while using a capital letter "M" I am speaking of the species of Man. The wo at the beginning of the word woman is an affix which is descriptive of the type of Man you are. An affix placed before a word changes its meaning and gives it direction. The meaning of woman, wo–man, is "Man with womb." When I speak of a man in a certain context without a capital "M" I am speaking of the male of the species of Man. A prefix changes the meaning of the word or makes it more specific. That's how the English language works.

All Men, no matter the colour of your skin or geographical base are born free and equal with unalienable rights. This means we have rights given to us by a higher power than ourselves. The rights of life, liberty and property. Your rights end where another's begin which means while enjoying your rights you must not infringe on the rights of others.

If you were born with obligations to other Men to follow the rules of their society that would mean you have been born into slavery. This is against our most fundamental freedoms and a violation of our unalienable rights given to us by our Creator. Are we born into slavery? The answer is no. That would be the most horrendous crime not only against Man but a crime against God. We are all the children of the Creator. How would you feel if somebody kidnapped your children and threw them in prison to be abused and mistreated?

So then what gives the authority to the authorities? You do.

"God is no respecter of persons." is a famous bible quote that may not make sense until you define what kind of person you are. I am not talking about the quality of your character but rather what contracts you may have with other Men.

We have all come to know of ourselves as people, I am a person, but what does that mean? The word person is a very vague term. There are many different types of persons. When we speak of ourselves as a person we usually mean natural person which is the flesh and blood Man. However the origin of the word comes from the word persona which according to Black's Law Dictionary comes from Roman Law and means "A person; an individual human being." This might make perfect sense to you because after all you're a human being aren't you? I then ask you since we now know what affixes do, that they change the meaning of words, what type of being is a hu-man being?

One of the many types of persons according to Black's Law Dictionary Ninth Edition is as follows: "artificial person. An entity, such as a corporation, created by law and given certain legal rights and duties of a human being; a being real or imaginary, who for the purpose of legal reasoning is treated more or less as a human being."

If you were born here on earth and are a child of the Creator you are first in line. You are an Original Native of Mother Earth which means you have all the rights bestowed upon you by your Creator. If, however, you contract with another Man to join their society and play by their rules than that is your free will and must be respected. What this means is that it is your right to surrender all your God given unalienable rights and enter into a contract with another Man for benefits and privileges within their society or organization. In exchange for these benefits and privileges you must play by their rules or suffer the consequences. This is what gives the authorities their authority, they authored it. They wrote the rules of their society which you joined of your own free will, it's their game, they own it.

This brings us to contract law. If you enter into a contract with another Man you come to an agreement of the parties. We do this all the time in our daily lives. If you work for somebody else such as a cook at a restaurant you have submitted an application which is a request to contract with the owners of the restaurant who are represented by the manager who has the authority to hire you. You are willing to exchange your time and energy in exchange for benefits and privileges which is money, your paycheck. When entering this contract you are given a title such as cook which is a form of rank, which determines the amount of authority you have within the business structure. While in the kitchen if you are a cook you must answer to the chef because the title of chef gives a person a higher rank within that system. The chef has authority over the cooks and the manager has authority over the chef. This is an agreement of the parties. While you are in the kitchen these ranks must be respected or there will be consequences.

Does this mean the chef can tell the cooks what to do after work in their own personal lives? No, of course not because the cook is no longer acting in the capacity of the cook, they finished their shift and now revert back to the capacity of a Man and all Men are created equal. At the beginning of their next shift they once again assume the rank of cook and must answer to the chef. Their rank as cook is an artificial person.

The word person can mean several different things but the

way contract law works is this. All Men are created equal but if you are willing to surrender your rank as an Original Native and contract with another Man you are no longer equals. This is where the artificial person comes into play. The artificial person allows us to surrender our authority to another Man's authority in exchange for benefits and privileges. This is a good thing. It allows us to enter into an agreement and assume a status or rank within the system. It is not who we are but a tool we use for business.

The artificial person is created the instant you contract with another and agree to do as they say or have authority over them. It is not who we are. It is not our identity but we assume liability while acting in the capacity of the given rank within the agreement. The cook answers to the chef.

In this system Men are not equal. They have ranks and titles within the system and some Men have authority over others. If you are the cook that is your status or rank within the system. This is why God is no respecter of persons because acting in the status or rank of a legal person you have surrendered your authority to another which is your right to do so, and must be respected.

If you join a society where your rank is an Aboriginal you have willingly accepted and applied for this rank in exchange for benefits and privileges. This brings us once again back to affixes. Are you normal or are you abnormal? Are you present or are you absent? Are you the Original or are you Aboriginal? If you are the Original you have the right to self-rule as long as you obey the laws of Origin or Natural Law which can be summed up with these simple rules.

"Do unto others as you would have them do unto you."

"Do no harm."

"Be good."

If you are claiming to be an Aboriginal you are claiming that you are not the Original. This is why there are Aboriginal reservations. You don't need a reservation to stay in a house that you own. If you wish to stay in the house of another, like a hotel, you need a reservation. This is why the government of Canada gives so much money funding Aboriginal awareness. You have been tricked into claiming that you are not the Original. Aboriginal, abnormal, absent. Who are you? What is your status within the system?

Whatever your status is within the system you are bound by it's laws and in Canada they call them acts and statutes. What are acts and statutes anyway? These are nothing more than corporate policies of the corporation of Canada and they only apply to government employees, citizens, residents and members of the democracy of Canada.

An act or to act involves an actor portraying an event but it is not the event itself, merely a re-creation of it. A statute or statue is a representation of real life but not life itself. The statue of David is not David himself but merely a representation of him. These things are replicas of real life but not life itself, they're imitations of the real thing. Acts and statutes are not real laws but corporate policies that apply to those involved in their system. They are imitations of laws.

"All the world's a stage." Shakespeare knew exactly what was going on.

Canada

In order to know what Canada is you must first determine which Canada you are talking about. Are you referring to the landmass located within the geographical borders commonly referred to as Canada? Are you referring to the democratic society of Canada? Or are you referring to the corporation of Canada?

No matter what Canada you are talking about it is the property of "Her Majesty the Queen." Most people believe that the Queen is only a figurehead but if you have ever read The Consolidation of the Canadian Constitution Acts 1867 to 1982 it clearly states at the top of the document "Copyright Her Majesty the Queen in Right of Canada"

The Constitution Act was formerly known as the British North American Act. One can only assume why they changed the name, to make it less obvious we are all British subjects under British rule.

We have been British subjects since the British first came here and slaughtered the Original Natives of this land and they are still doing it. "A British subject I was born, a British subject I will die." - John A. Macdonald – first prime minister of Canada.

When somebody holds the copyright it means they are the author which makes them the authority. This means it is yours and you own it. If you hold the copyright of a book it means you own the rights to it. You are the authority on that piece of literature and your authority is protected by law. Nobody can duplicate the book without permission or change it to suit their own wishes. If you are not the author you have no authority.

This principal can be supported by Natural or Original Law in the following way. If you write a book and wish to sell it for profit it is your God given right to do so. If however someone else decides to copy your book and sell it for their own profit they are causing you harm because they have stolen your work, which is a result of your time and energy. This will affect your profits, money, which is a representation of other people's time and energy, therefore they are stealing your energy. If you wish to reproduce or alter the book you must first get permission from the author and pay a fee to the author or authority called a "royalty".

The government of Canada is a service provided by the corporation of Canada which is owned by the Queen. They actually call some of their government buildings Service Canada. It is a business that offers a service and the service is to govern the people and their land. So why the hell are we hiring somebody from a foreign country to rule us? Good question. Here's how that works. It starts with the Statement of Live Birth.

In Ontario we call it a statement of live birth, in other parts of Canada and around the world it has different names but whatever you call it, it is the same thing. It is the form your mother fills out to register your birth with the government. This document has your mother's signature on it. They are not registering the child they are registering the event of a live birth. This is done when you are only days old. To register the event is just to keep a record of it.

After you have filled out the Statement of Live Birth the government will send you a birth certificate which is where all the problems come from. On the front of the birth certificate is the seal of the Register General with their signature as well as the signature of the Deputy Registrar General and claims to be a certified extract from the birth registration which is very misleading. They extract the information from the statement of live birth only. On the Government website where you can order a copy of your birth certificate they even have the two listed as a "Short form birth certificate" and a "Long form birth certificate" which implies they are two different versions of the same thing which is not the case.

The "Statement of Live Birth" has your mother's signature on it with no government seal on it and the "Short Form Birth Certificate" has the seal of the Registrar General on it with signatures of the government. When you order the "Long form birth certificate" you will receive a document filled out by your mother with a black box consisting of two lines around it and on the outside of that box you will see the stamp of the Registrar General as well as the signature of the Deputy Registrar General. The black box indicates a document within a document. Everything on the inside of the box is the document your mother was given to fill out.

Everything on the outside of the box is a separate document that was added later by the government. This is clearly evident because the signature of the Deputy Registrar General will be different depending on who was in office at the time of ordering the certificate. This is done to validate it as an official and legitimate copy of the original.

    Your name is your property. That is why they call it your given name, it was given to you, it is yours, you own it. What your mother did when she filled out the statement of live birth was she registered the event of your birth that included your name with the government and in return you got a birth certificate. What the short form birth certificate represents is another kind of birth, the birth of a legal person.

    Corporations can not recognize a Man because they are in different jurisdictions. There needs to be an established title. This brings us back to contract law. All Men are created equal. Corporations can only do business with other corporations where ranks and titles have been established. The cook answers to the chef. The birth certificate is a legal person which is a corporation. When we do anything under the birth certificate we are acting as an agent or employee of the corporation. Although the birth certificate has what appears to be your name on it, it is written in all capital letters while on the statement of live birth or "long form birth certificate" only the first letters in your name are capitalized. What does this mean? Let's use some logic and deductive reasoning to figure this out.

    The statement of live birth has your mother's signature on it with your name on it. It is a recording of an event that happened between you and your mother. You and your mother authored it. That event is yours, it belongs to you. You own it.

    The birth certificate has a replica of your name on it spelled in all capital letters with the governments seal on it and with two government signatures on it. They authored it, they have the authority over this legal person, they own it. The birth certificate is government property. It is a corporation owned by Her Majesty the Queen. It only has what appears to be your name on it. This is just like when a certain fast food chain had 100% Beef written on their hamburger wrappers when the actual meat was not 100% beef, it was the name of the company. The name of the corporation was "100% Beef" but they were serving horse meat.

It is like playing a board game. If someone comes over to your house to play Monopoly you are given a game piece such as a race car or top hat to use while playing the game but the piece does not belong to you it belongs to whoever owns the game. The person that brings the board game to your house is obligated to give you a game piece because it is your house and you have a right to play or not play if you wish. While playing the game you are acting in the capacity of a player and are subject to all the rules of the game. Go directly to jail, do not pass go, do not collect $200. That's what the birth certificate is, a means to play in their game.

The birth certificate is an offer to contract. In order for it to have any effect you must first accept it and use it.

When you apply for a Social Insurance Number you are submitting an application to work not only in Canada but for Canada. You are applying for the opportunity to work for the corporation of the legal person that shares a version of your name but is owned by the government. The position you are applying for is "Taxpayer"

"The taxpayer – that's someone who works for the government that doesn't have to take the civil service examination" - Ronald Reagan former president of the United States of America.

People think that being a taxpayer is a good thing. They convince themselves they are making their contribution to society. They should be asking themselves where are the profits from the sales of all our natural resources?

We now know Canada is a corporation owned by someone from a foreign land called "Her Majesty the Queen" and declares herself to be "royalty". You are working for the corporation of Canada through the legal person owned by "Her Majesty the Queen" with a Social Insurance Number. Just because you have been given a birth certificate does not mean you are acting under it. Just like if someone comes to your house and offers you a game piece it does not mean you are actually playing. You must first willingly join the game.

Working under the Social Insurance Number and paying taxes is what makes you a taxpayer. You are an agent of the Queen. You have applied for the job. The cook answers to the chef.

The democracy of governments is nothing more than a distraction. They are giving people the illusion of freedom while serving the corporations. This is how they keep us willing slaves unaware of who we are. They make us think that if you vote you can make a difference when the only choices that exist in their system are the lesser of many evils. A vote for the lesser of evils is still evil. While belonging to a democracy you are wilfully surrendering power of attorney of your life to another. You will do as they say and they make the rules.

The Queen or rather the office of Her Majesty the Queen holds the copyright and is the author of Canada making the office of the Queen the authority. She has the right to delegate responsibilities to whoever she wants. This includes police. I am not against having peace officers to keep people safe but what we have now are corporate policy enforcers. They do uphold the laws of Canada and are supposed to help people, but they also do so much harm and destroy so many people's lives for non-crimes.

I know of this first hand because they raided my property, stole my crop, kidnapped me and threw me in prison where I was horribly mistreated. I didn't do anything wrong. I was growing a couple large crops of marijuana at the time but I wasn't hurting anybody. For there to be a real crime there must first be an injured party. If there is no injured party there is no crime. At the time I was unaware that the reason these acts and statutes applied to me is because I asked for it. I didn't think I had a choice, I thought this was just how things were done. I did not know what freedom was but I know now and I'm telling everybody. This is my revenge. This is justice.

In order for you to become a taxpayer or a member of the democracy you must first declare yourself a Canadian citizen. If you are a citizen of Canada it is assumed that you have taken the citizenship oath which reads as follows.

> I swear (or affirm)
> That I will be faithful
> And bear true allegiance
> To Her Majesty Queen Elizabeth the
> Second
> Queen of Canada
> Her Heirs and Successors
> And that I will faithfully observe
> The laws of Canada
> And fulfil my duties as a Canadian citizen.

I have never in my life taken such an oath however almost all documents that the government wants us to fill out ask if we are a Canadian citizen and I have always checked the box indicating I was. I was always told I was a Canadian citizen, I thought I was born a citizen. I did not understand what it really meant.

Taking this oath means you have given everything to the Queen including your rights, body, and all other property. It means you swear to be their slave and blindly obey their corporate policies and fulfil your duties whatever they may be. It means the Queen owns you and you are a British subject because you are subject to British rule. You are subject to all their acts and statutes that can be changed at will with no basis in law. You are pledging your life to the corporation. If you have never wilfully taken this oath it still applies to you if you claim to be a citizen. It is assumed that you know what being a citizen entails. In reality it is fairly close to making a deal with the devil because it moves you away from God. You have given up your God given rights to belong to a society of psychopaths.

Being a member of their democracy, being a taxpayer, and being a citizen. This is the trinity of trickery used to enslave us.

Freedom

One of our unalienable God given rights is the right to NOT be associated with something or someone that we don't want to be associated with. If I were to start my own society and I wanted people to join, they would have to do so of their own free will. If I were to force somebody to be a member of my society by kidnapping them and throwing them in prison as well as stealing their children and all their worldly possessions if they refused to join, that would be wrong. It is called slavery. The most horrendous crime against Man is to steal his life. That is what prison is, they are taking a portion of your life from you.

Life, Liberty and Property. These are rights given to us by God and no Man has the right to take them from us.

Just as I cannot force you to join my society the government cannot force you to join their society. If they say you have to get a drivers licence and you have to get a social insurance number if you want certain permissions in Canada they would be right. But which Canada are they talking about?

The democracy of Canada is a joke, I don't want to be a part of that anymore so I can just fill out the forms or send them notice that I no longer wish to belong to their democracy.

The corporation of Canada? Well if you are working at a job you don't like is it not your right to quit? Acting under the social insurance number is a job with the title of taxpayer which makes you an employee of a foreign corporation. I don't want to work for you anymore so I think I will just send my notice to Revenue Canada that I quit and stop paying taxes.

Being a Canadian citizen means you are a slave. Renounce your unspoken oath.

Do you mean the landmass commonly referred to as Canada? Well now let's get something straight. I am an Original Native of this land, equal to all other Men. I was born here therefor I have the right to be here. In my status of Original Native I outrank all governments. God created Man, Man created government. The creator is always greater than the created. In my status of an

Original Native the only obligations I was born with are to God to be a good steward of the earth and to love and respect my fellow Man. I roam where I please as long as I do not trespass and do no harm. My rights end where another's begin. If I have no contracts with other Men then nobody has authority over me but God.

Are you a resident of Canada? Do you reside within the jurisdiction on Canada? You can become a non-resident of Canada and they cannot make you move if you have no association or contract with them. Remember, the government of Canada is a foreign owned company. You are the Original Native. This is your house.

If you return all of your government ID such as drivers licence, health card, social insurance number and any other form of government identification that would leave you with only the birth certificate which is a corporation owned by the government with what would appear to be your name on it. When you are acting as an agent or employee of the birth certificate you are also acting as a surety which means you are assuming liability for it. It is not you nor is it your property, it is a piece of their game they are tricking you to use and assume liability for. That's why good gardeners go to prison.

Now that you know the birth certificate does not belong to you and it's not really your name on it but only an imitation of your name like their acts and statutes are imitations of law then you come to realize something else which can either be liberating or terrifying. If I used government ID to open my bank account and acted as an employee or agent on behalf of the legal person/corporation which is owned by the Queen. Does this make my bank account government property?

Logic and reason would say yes. As it turns out you have been very generous to our British rulers because all this money you have been earning for a legal person which is a corporation owned by the Queen has never been yours. This is how they can seize people's bank accounts if you break their corporate rules and regulations. They are not stealing your money, they are taking their money. They let you manage the account of the legal person because you are the employee of the legal person/corporation. This keeps the illusion up and the game going. What gives their money value anyway? We do. It used to be backed by gold but now they just create ones and zeros out of thin air. This is the reason why they want to get rid of cash. To force you to play in their system.

The good news of this is that for all of you who are in debt, the debt belongs to the legal person as well. Although while you are a taxpaying member of the democracy and a citizen you are liable for all debt you could just quit the democracy and quit acting as a taxpayer. Give them back their corporation and let them pay the debt, after all it is their corporation. Did you swear your life to the Queen by becoming a citizen? Make it clear you are not a citizen and your life belongs to you.

And what if you own your house that took you thirty years to pay off and you want to leave the society of Canada? Does the legal person own your house? That is a tricky one which may take some thought. Let's look at it from both sides shall we.

One could argue that yes it is Government property because everything was done under the legal person. As a matter of fact you could say that since the Queen owns the legal person, the corporation represented by the birth certificate and you have been acting as an agent or employee of the Queen your house is actually a government office. Maybe this is why they can kick in your door for growing marijuana. They don't consider it to be your house so much as another government office. This is the sad truth if you are a taxpayer. One of the lowest ranks in their system.

If you look at it from the other side you could say yes it is my house. I was under the understanding that I owned this property and had no idea I have been working for the corporation of the legal person with an imitation of my name on it as represented by the birth certificate. The details of the contract were not disclosed to me. There was not full disclosure. You were acting in bad faith which makes the contract null and void. This may be the case but are you willing to bet the farm on it?

If the government did try to seize your assets if you tried to leave their system that would be to obvious and their scam would be exposed for what it is which would cause the fall of their society. If they refuse to let you leave than you are a political prisoner. If they say the house was never yours but the property of the corporation, which they would never do, you could just tell them... "As an Original Native I claim this land."

Life, Liberty, and Property. These are God given rights that cannot be denied to us by any other man unless we have wilfully submitted our authority to them.

So since you are an Original Native and it is your God given right to property how come you are stuck living in a place you do not own or you had to work hard for many years to pay for? Because you don't know who you are.

In Canada there is plenty of "crown" land. Most people understand this to be government land. The government of Canada is a business that is supposed to take care of our affairs for us in exchange for a paycheck. This is comparable to the manager of the restaurant that manages the restaurant for the owners. He has been given the "authority" by the owners because they are the ones that created or authored the business. The manager holds a higher rank than the chef and the cook and outranks them within this system. They are not equals. The manager must answer to the owners because they have the authority to fire them.

Who are you in this scenario?

The land belongs to you and you belong to the land. You are the owner. The problem is that the manager we got stuck with, the government, is a criminal. They have put a spell over us, and by that I mean their bullshit legal language or "spelling". They have made us forget we are the owners. They then offered us a job which is working for their legal person that is a corporation that they own and has a replica of your name on it.

Do not think of the birth certificate as anything more than what it is, a job offer. Help wanted, apply within. And you did apply didn't you. You applied for a Social Insurance Number and received the title of "taxpayer". A rank so low within their system it is equivalent to calling yourself an Aboriginal. Aboriginal or Unoriginal, same difference. So who has given them the authority over you and this land? You. Who can take it back? You. But only in the capacity or rank as an Original Native. The manager answers to the owner, not the cook.

What would this mean? It would mean you are free. Of course they do not want us to be free. The police would need to be educated about the rights of Man and the limits of their authority. They can keep their human rights, I claim the rights of Man. They have tricked us not only with the word Aboriginal getting people to claim to NOT be an Original, they have also tricked us in to claiming to be a hu-man being. Hu-man, sub-man...the fall of Man.

The human being is the legal person as represented by the birth certificate. It is not who you are, it is an artificial person that they own. It means something different to us but within their system they can change the definition of words at will. It's all in the spelling. We have all been put under a "spell" by the Evil Queen. The Originals have been tricked into getting a Social Insurance Number. The Original SIN that has brought the world to the state it is now in.

Man is a being but you would never say "Man being" would you? What is the Man being? If you put a prefix in front of the word Man to describe the type of Man you are talking about you are changing the word to be more specific. That is why when you claim to be a human being you are actually claiming to be a being that is like Man but not a Man. Hu-man being, sub-man being. The paper monster that has swallowed the world.

If everybody stops paying taxes, or royalties, where will all the government services come from?

We all own the natural resources of this land together. Every Man that was born within the borders of the land has an even share. Canada is one of the richest countries of the world when it comes to natural resources. That is where our funding for government services is supposed to come from. They are all being stolen from us by big corporations and have been replaced with a new resource, the human resource. They are hiding nothing from us you just need to open your eyes.

Forestry, fishing, mining... it's all being stolen. Our natural resources would be not only be enough to pay for government services, we would all be getting a cheque in the mail every month from the government for our share of the surplus if it wasn't all being stolen.

For an example let's take forestry. All the trees in "Canada" belong to all of the Original natives equally with the exception of private property. If a company wanted to harvest the lumber off of government managed crown land they would have to buy the trees with the money going to a non-corrupt limited government to spend on government services with the rest being dispersed to the people. Any Original Native wanting to start a business and harvest more than their fair share would have to first get permission and pay for what they take. If any foreign companies would want to buy the rights to mine or develop a timber mill in Canada that would be fine as long as they follow our procedures to ensure they are not hurting the environment and they pay a fair price for what they take. Do you have any idea how rich our country would be if all our natural resources weren't being stolen from us? There would be no poverty, no homeless, no one would ever go hungry. There would be no unemployment, no begging the government for handouts. We would be living in a paradise.

When it comes to land ownership it is a concept that is totally against Natural Law, like everything else the governments around the world do. We don't own the land, we belong to it. We come from the Earth and one day we will return to it. It is our God given duty to be good stewards of our Mother Earth. We must respect our Mother and protect her from those that would harm her. As an Original Native of Mother Earth you have a right to live in peace and harvest whatever crops you wish as long as you do no harm.

The crown land here in Canada is commonly referred to as government land, which is incorrect. The government is just the manager of the land with the Original Natives being the owners/stewards. Since we have all surrendered our rights to the government we no longer have any claim to the land. God is no respecter of persons. Everything is tied to the legal person represented by the birth certificate. When you apply for licences you needed government identification. When you register to vote you needed government identification. This was to make sure you worked for the legal person which is a corporation owned by the Queen. They had to make sure you were employed by their system and a citizen where you wilfully surrendered your rights for benefits and privileges. All you have to do is quit. Once you have quit working for them and claim your title of Original Native you are now acting in the capacity of the owner. You can fire them.

I quit, you're fired. It's just that simple.

Then you could lawfully return to the land and live without any government interference. You could claim a piece of land to work and do whatever you wish to make a living. You could have a huge garden and grow all the organic vegetables and marijuana you could ever want. You could probably make a lot of money at it as well without the government to bring you down. You must not claim stewardship over to large of an area because the land belongs to everybody, we have to share.

If you wish to grow a plant given to us by God that is your right as long as it does not cause harm. If you open a methamphetamine lab and start dealing hard core drugs that cause harm you would be breaking Natural Law and must be held liable for your actions. This is why we need peace officers and courts. People would be less likely to do harmful acts if they were not desperate. If everybody was allowed to be free they would not be forced to commit harmful acts in order to survive. Everybody would have something to loose. Every Original would have their own plot of land to work and benefit from. We would help each other by working together to build housing for everybody. There would be no theft because people would have everything they need. There would be no poverty. There would be no hunger. There would be no homeless. It would be... paradise. The garden of Origin.

Let me spell it out for you.

We were the Originals until we applied for a Social Insurance Number often referred to as a SIN number. From this time on we have been exiled from the garden of Origin. I think I have heard this story before...

We have all been swindled, God damn the Queen.

The time has come for the Original Natives to stand up and claim our rights. We are on the dawn of a new age.

The time has come for the Rise of Man.

Declaration of Independence

With God as my witness, I _____ being an Original Native of Mother Earth, flesh and blood Man of God, hereby declare my independence from the government of Canada and Her Majesty the Queen. I withdraw my consent to be associated with the Canadian government, Her Majesty the Queen or any other political body in any way shape or form. I no longer agree to act as a taxpayer or agent of Canada. I am not a resident of Canada. I am not a member of the democracy of Canada. I no longer work for the corporation of Canada through the corporation of the birth certificate with a replica of my good God given name on it. I renounce the oath of citizenship and allegiance to the Queen and all Her Heirs and Successors on the grounds of trickery and deceit.

It is against my conscience to support such a corrupt government that acts without honour and routinely commits crimes against Man, Beast, and Mother Earth. I hereby declare due to the corruption of the Canadian government and Her Majesty the Queen all contracts and agreements between myself and the Canadian government and Her Majesty the Queen to be null and void. I am no longer a Canadian citizen that is subject to the acts, statutes or policies of Canada, answering only to God and my fellow Man in an agreement to live a peaceful life and do no harm.

_____ Original Native, Man of God

If you sign a declaration of independence without having the knowledge to back it up you may spend a very long time in prison. Even if you do know how to defend your rights, the system is so corrupt you must have an insurance policy. The best insurance policy you can have is to be as vocal as you can be and speak the truth. God will take care of the rest.

If you resort to violence they will label you a terrorist in the eyes of the people. Your best weapon is a camera. Be loud, stand proud.

The New World

The corruption of governments must stop. There is only one way that this is going to happen. You must stop feeding the beast. Stop giving it your energy. Give back to Cesar what is Cesar's and walk away. I am speaking of course of the legal person. This must be done in a peaceful manner. You must educate people around you about freedom.

"Father forgive them for they know not what they do." this is a Quote of Jesus Christ during his crucifixion.

When the police who believe they have the right to kidnap you and throw you in prison they are right if you belong to their system. It is your duty to communicate with and educate the police and government on all levels on the rights of Man and make them aware they no longer have any authority over you in the capacity of a police officer that is really only a corporate policy enforcer. It is important to understand we all have the capacity and duty to act as a "Peace Officer" which means to keep the peace and interfere when there is harm being done.

If you have done everything properly and dissolved all contracts with them they will still drag you into court and try to trick you into acting as an agent for the legal person and a citizen as long as the birth certificate still exists. When this happens, and it might, you let the judge (actor wearing a dress) know.

"As God as my witness I am here as an Original Native, Man of God. I am here against my will. I have harmed no Man and broken no contract. I am not an agent for any corporation nor am I a citizen. I assume no liability. My life belongs to God, not you. You have no authority over me. It is my will to leave immediately." Then walk away, don't ask their permission, you don't need it, just walk away.

Before you leave the jurisdiction of Canada you must first understand these concepts and be able to defend your rights.

So for all those marijuana farmers out there I suggest you learn your rights and fully prepare yourself before you go out and do this. No matter how well you know your rights it is your duty to educate the police in your area and around the world. If you are growing marijuana and hiding it like you are doing something wrong then you are acting like a criminal so they will treat you like one. However, if you educate law enforcement and inform them that you are no longer a part of their society in any way shape or form and that their corporate policies no longer apply to you, you will be lawfully in the right. Let them know your intentions are to grow as much marijuana as you like and it's none of their concern because they no longer have any authority over you. Then you are acting in good faith and doing the honourable thing. Be as public as you can possibly be. Let everyone know what your intentions are and that you are exercising your God given rights, will not infringe on the rights of others and do no harm.

Think of it like this. If you are an Original Native of Mother Earth that has no contract with any Man that has done no harm and a group of armed individuals that work for a foreign monarchy kicks in your door, steals your property and kidnaps you at gunpoint, this would be an act of war. You have just been invaded by a foreign corporation owned by Her Majesty the Queen that resides overseas.

They can do that to taxpayers, citizens and members of the democracy because there is an existing contract where they have submitted authority over themselves to another.

If they do this to an Original Native with no existing contracts between them it would be the equivalent of you kicking in the cops door and stealing their property, kidnapping them at gunpoint and locking them up in your basement. If you were to try to do this you would be shot and rightfully so.

It is our God given right and duty to defend ourselves against this sort of behaviour. If you have acted in good faith and left the jurisdiction of Canada entirely and have alerted the police to what is going on because you don't want any misunderstandings... Then you grow a crop and they invade you and try to steal it and kidnap you... well. You would be well within your rights to defend yourself by whatever means necessary, warrant or no warrant, as long as you have caused no harm. If you have somebody locked up in your basement than you have caused harm and they would be well within their rights to kick in your door, not as police officers but as peace officers. If you are just growing a crop and have caused no harm they have no right to interfere with your life.

It would be the equivalent to one country invading another country with the intention of stealing their property and kidnapping their people. It is no different. The police of Canada work for and serve Her Majesty the Queen and if you are a taxpaying citizen, so do you. Not only do you serve the Queen and are a British subject, you have assumed one of the lowest ranks in the system, the rank of a taxpaying citizen that has sworn their life to the Queen. This is why the police can kidnap you for nonviolent crimes with no injured party. They are not kidnapping the Man who holds the rank of Original Native, Child of the Creator, they are arresting persons, legal persons. God is no respecter of persons.

They will say that marijuana harms people but we all know that is not true. For a crime to take place you need an injured party. Who is the plaintiff? The cop? You didn't harm the cop, the cop harmed you. If anything you could sue the cops for terrorizing you and stealing your property. Marijuana has tremendous healing and therapeutic properties which is why it is illegal in the first place because our governments are owned by corporations like the big pharmaceutical cartels.

We can't change Canada because it does not belong to us. If we want to be free we have to give up being Canadian. We must tell the Queen to take her constitution and her country and fuck off. You must go back to your status of Original Native of Mother Earth. Give up your patriotic pride and go back to God. This concept applies to governments around the world.

That in a nutshell is the story of your enslavement and the keys to freedom. Although I live in Canada it applies to all governments. We are all Original Natives of Mother Earth. We can all go back to our Original status at any time. We owe it to ourselves. We owe it to our children.

The world is going to hell and this is how we can save it. Do not protest. People who protest the government are just unhappy slaves. When you protest you are whining to your government masters to do something that you should be doing yourself. If you want to change the world for the better the only way to do that is for you to stop being so dependent on the government and govern yourself. Stop feeding the beast and let it die. All you have to do is walk away.

From death comes new life. You must return to the Garden from which you came. Go back to the Land of Origin.

My Name is Patrick Westley Devlin, Original Native of Mother Earth, Man of God.

Who are you?

www.ingramcontent.com/pod-product-compliance
Lightning Source LLC
Chambersburg PA
CBHW071827200526
45169CB00018B/1141